Reluctant Care

poems by

Michael McDermott

Finishing Line Press
Georgetown, Kentucky

Reluctant Care

ACKNOWLEDGMENTS

Bourgeon: Pas de Deux

Publisher: Leah Maines
Editor: Christen Kincaid
Author Photo: Chris McDermott
Cover Design: Juanita Barnett

Printed in the USA on acid-free paper.
Order online: www.finishinglinepress.com
                 also available on amazon.com

Author inquiries and mail orders:
Finishing Line Press
P. O. Box 1626
Georgetown, Kentucky 40324
U. S. A.

Table of Contents

For Chris, Erin, and Kelly

Washington Hospital Center: Burn Unit

1

Mom arrived at the hospital by chopper long before
we did. A trip of a lifetime no one wanted, a trip I
could not imagine, could not fathom, except for
the fact that I was part of it, part of the why

that I didn't understand, part of the way
she lived, and now part of how she'd die.
All I wanted to do was to help, to say
that I loved her and to hear the answer tie

things together neatly for me. How were we here
now, in an unimaginable place, real only
in bad television dramas with their ads for beer
to break the tension and keep the lonely

feeling happy? What were we doing here now?
Who was doing this to us, Lord? Why here now?

2

The doctor had horn-rimmed glasses and wore
a blue blazer at two o'clock in the morning.
He talked to us in quiet gentle tones, warning
with statistics, calculating probabilities that tore
the skin of confusion away revealing a raw reality:
take the percentage of third-degree coverage—
Mom's was thirty-six percent coverage—
then add in age for the probability of mortality.

My brother Tim and I did the math as we stood outside
her room. A nurse moved silently about her bed.
Sixty-five years plus thirty-six percent equaled . . . .
As morning light emerged, we took turns by her side,
then each took a break away from the bed,
away from the room, away from the clock.

3

Three days. Time sputters and blurs,
three days of morning, noon, and night,
three days of unbelievable denial, of words
unspoken, of fluid therapies that might

work, but, then, don't. Then systems fail
and the fluids begin to spill over into swollen
hands, feet, and finally the face, so pale,
becomes unrecognizable in its dimension.

The pace around her quickens and we back
out of the way until the doctor comes to talk.
Death is so close I can almost see it, but I lack
the skill to fight it, lack the weapons to lock

it out of the room so the doctor can win
the final battle which the doctor must win.

4

And then the doctor comes to talk. He wants,
we think at first, to pull the plug. "No. We,
we just couldn't do . . . ." "No," he says. He wants
to try one more trick, and we breathe, relieved.

Activity begins again to move around her.
Knobs adjusted, IVs flicked, quiet comments
and instructions. A new instrument, torn from a paper
wrap, is quickly employed. Then, the resident

by the heart monitor taps its glass screen
with his finger, an empty thumping. He speaks
over his shoulder, points at the still green

grid, and finally shifts his eyes to the clock.

First, there was the time before Mom died.
Then, there was the time after Mom died.

5

I don't remember the drive home.
Tim says it is something he'll never forget.
He said he cried his eyes out, yet
I did not, for the whole drive home,
I did not. Within sight of the Capitol's dome
where Constitution Ave. and N. Capitol met,
I remember, dreamlike—the car stops, I get
out, then Tim takes over the drive home.

I remember only walking around the car
beneath a street lamp in the dark still city,
but that's it. I don't remember why
we needed to switch drivers, or stop the car,
or what we said driving out of the city,
or, even, at that time of night . . . why.

Dad's Fault

It was, of course, Dad's fault
that Mom fell asleep
on the sofa, cigarette burning,
while, once again,
like a beached whale, he
lay washed ashore
in a hospital
drying out.

If he had been home,
he could have pissed
on the fire
and put it out.

Reluctant Care

After the fire.
After Mom died.
After Dad dried out.
He lived away
in a group home.
Away from the reality
that he was, indeed,
part of the family,
but a paterfamilias
without the respect.

After a year,
for convenience,
I moved him
to an apartment
about ten minutes
away from my home.
"A little place of my own,"
Dad said. For me,
the theater for a ten-year run
of "Reluctant Care."

Two Rocks

Like two rocks,
procrastination and resentment
guarded the route
to Dad's apartment.

If procrastination didn't force
me to miss even leaving my house,
then the whirlpool
of resentment would wrap
about me like a storm wind
whipping up howls
of self-indulgent wails
until I would gurgle down
into a pit,
get into
my car
and
drive
to
Dad's.

Fixing Dad's TV

I am driving to Dad's
to fix his television.

It is broken
only in terms
of confused remotes
plunged out of sequence
by a reason eclipsed
from slow recognition,
constantly denied,
that the pieces of the world
no longer fit
as they did.

This disintegration
is revealed
on the nightly news
where it is clear as a bell
that the world is going to hell.

That's when Dad
pushed the wrong remote
causing him to call me
in desperation
to come and fix the TV, son.
Reset the damn thing so
the world can make sense again.

Fixing Dad's TV—Part 2

I arrive at Dad's apartment
and walk in as if I lived there.
In a way I do. I buy the groceries,
hit the place with a vacuum,
fix faucets, and close windows
stuck open from a feeble try
weeks earlier and forgotten
until the cold came visiting.
A reluctant home I suppose,
a place to which
I count the minutes
it takes before I get there;
a place where on the elevator,
I hope the time spent
will move just a little faster;
a place where I meet time
in ways I've never wished to know.

"I'm here," I announce
as I walk straight back
to the bedroom where
I see this odd fantastic
comic book character:
an old man holding
two Star Trek phasers
blasting away at the cycloptic invader
beaming flickering rays
of unheld horizontal snow.

"Fix this damn thing,"
was Dad's greeting,
mutually male
in its sweet rapport.
I stepped to the bedside
ignoring the spectacle
of splayed legs

unencumbered by clothing
except for the ever-present
threadbare robe not covering
anything at the moment,
and took the two instruments of destruction.

"Be careful," he said.
"You have to do it just right."
He had instructions.
But I ignored all
and just turned everything off.

"NO!!" Dad screamed.
"You can't just . . ."
I turned them back on in sequence,
first the TV,
then the VCR,
and they worked fine.

Dad smiled beatifically,
"Thank you son,"
then frowned,
"Don't go yet."
He needed to make sure
that all was as it should be,
that the channels in the TV guide
matched the channels on the TV.

All was fine and I could do no wrong
until the next time something went wrong.

Grocery Shopping: The List

—Red Delicious apples, six
—D'Anjou pears, six
—salad from the salad bar

> "You got my list?"
> "I think I have everything."
> "Apples?"
> "I've got the list, Dad."

—cut fresh fruit and vegetables in plastic packs
—fruit cocktail, six pull-top cans
—apple sauce (w/ cinnamon), one jar

> "Apple sauce?"
> "I thought you'd like to try something new."
> "Why? . . . . Just get what I asked for."

—American cheese, 16 slices
—turkey baloney, 16 slices
—Dinty Moore stew, couple of cans

> "Make sure that's low fat turkey baloney."
> "Isn't that an oxymoron?
> "What?"

—Oreo cookies
—Triskets
—Wheat Thins

> "Triskets and Wheat Thins?"
> "Yes. Triskets and . . . ."
> "Why do you need both?"
> "Because I do. Just get them.

—bread, wheat
—cereal, 2 variety packs
—oatmeal, instant

> "Did I say bread?"
> "Yes, I got the bread."
> "What about the cereal?"
> "Yup, got the cereal."
> "Okay."

—Minute Maid orange juice, six cans
—skim milk
—coffee

> "Dad, how's your coffee?"
> "Got to go to the kitchen to check."
> "No, Dad. That'll take too long. I'll just get some." (Clunk)
> "Dad? Use the phone in the kitchen."
> "Dad? . . . Dad."

Haircut

The Saturday morning barbershop
is take-a-number packed,
with tow-headed boys and wrangling moms,
teenage toughs and military men
both in civvies, reading Field and Stream.
Someone always offers Dad a seat.

Barbershop sounds sing brief solos
amidst a continuo of clips and buzz.
Barbershop smells touch memories
that always reminds Dad of a story
about a guy in a barbershop long ago.
Dad's number is always called mid-story.

Dad gingerly shuffles to the barber chair,
steps up in slow motion then falls back
into squeaking well-worn leather.
Bub the barber, comb in pocket,
swivels the chair, "What'll it be?"
"Short on the sides, long on the top."

The cut-and-buzz takes five minutes.
The barber looks at me. We've done this before.
Dad steps down and aims toward the door
while I add a buck to Dad's quarter tip,
pay the bill and get to the door
just in time for Dad to shuffle by.

Barbershop sounds sing brief solos
amidst a continuo of clips and buzz.
Barbershop smells touch memories,
always reminds me of a story.

Pas de Deux

In our choreography, Dad and I
had three types of dance:
the shower, the stairs, and the car.
The shower's dance was a slow kabuki-

like affair, where each movement
was punctuated with a certain pose
that had its own philosophy of alpha
and omega for each shifting limb.

The stairs required an ancient respect
where I, the younger, preceded
in descent and followed in ascent,
to catch the fall that would eventually come.

The car became a prop and barrier
to hold and skirt, target and leave,
enter and exit, like the hat and pouring rain
that danced with Gene Kelly.

In our dances, I provided the support
while spinning around his unending
juggernaut always heading for a rail,
a wall, "Some damn thing to grab on to."

The Shower Dance

Left	hand	on the sink.
Right	hand	on my shoulder.
Right	leg	over the tub side.
Left	leg	follows over.

Left	hand	lifts from the sink.
Right	hand	holds a metal handle.
Right	leg	holds steady.
Left	leg	holds steady.

Talk

He washed from his head to his balls,
I scrubbed his back to his sagging ass.

We'd hand-off the Shower Massage
live with a gentle drenching rain

that soaked anything in its path
including whatever I had on that day.

My primary job, again, was to catch
him, if, God forbid, he ever fell.

Other than that, I held the spray
on his tree-trunk legs until a needed rinse.

After scores of showers with minimal talk,
he joked about the family jewels. I laughed

in spite of myself, how outrageous, how odd.
Fathers and sons didn't joke about such things,

and yet, amid the slapping water and sloshing
wash cloth, my Dad joked about the family jewels.

This broke the ice. And we began to talk,
astounded at how much we had in common.

Potential: A Sestina

Other than the collections of mostly junk mail,
there was little else "active" in Dad's living room
except for the stacks of magazines—Newsweek,
National Geographic, Air Force Times, and Life,
with the occasional initial issue that was "free,"
but then required subscription for the next few years.

These accumulations represented several years
of assiduous avoidance of deciding, even with the junk mail,
what should be kept and what tossed. Worse were the free
offers, which could have easily filled the tiny living room
with potentials and benefits certain to fulfill one's life.
All of this promise salted among the tragic covers of Newsweek.

Of course, he would have loved to have written for Newsweek,
or for any of the papers and magazines in which for years
he worked to get coverage for the Air Force, almost a life
time full of press releases, phone calls, and bundles of mail
sent out to get the holy grail of publicity: a story, some room
in a column, a pick up on the AP wire, a little airtime for free.

But nothing ever really panned out. Except for some small free
columns in the Douglas (WY) Budget, there was no Newsweek
that answered his call, no National Geographic with room
on the staff for one more writer regardless of the years
of experience, the talent, the expertise in executing a mail
campaign that could quite literally change your life.

As one who tries to write, at least occasionally, the life
of writing that Dad always envisioned, where he'd be free
from the vagaries of the workplace to work the mail
with a constant outpouring of pieces, articles indeed for Newsweek,
a stream of short stories, even a couple of novels over the years,
as one who tries to write, I knew the true meaning of this room.

These, of course, were not piles of magazines in a living room,
not heaps of decaying yellow pages, fading covers without a life,
not meaningless days that dissolved into lost months, then years.
No. These were piles of potential, articles to read in moments free
in a hectic schedule of preparing to write something for Newsweek
or National Geographic, before hurrying down to get the day's mail.

It was the mail that was critical to the job, and this room
filled with its stacks of Newsweeks, Air Force Times, and Life,
when a little time was free, this little room held the work of years.

Dad Visits the Doctor

We went to many doctors over the years,
the offices, all of them, were similar, it seemed.
The acute scent of cleansing alcohol mixed
with nurses' perfume greeted our nostrils
in an ironic hint of antiseptic things to come.

Dad's stage whispers let the waiting room know
his feelings about a three-month old article,
while I pulled out my file, like Mom's
notebook filled with family numbers before me,
and did the paperwork—birthday, accounts,
telephone, address, and, yes, social security.

When Dad was finally called for the exam,
I went too, the factual backup to his dementia tales,
such as, "I'm fine, really. Shouldn't even be here."
Of course, the crusty sapless logs that were his legs,
with a fungal fantasy for toenails and a Mardi Gras
confetti of dead-skin flakes on the floor
told a different story, often amazing enough
for the doctor to call in a colleague.

Nurses visited throughout the exam
and Dad never missed a beat to flirt.
They'd laugh at his old fart audacity, "Be gentle,"
as they strapped on the velcro pressure cuff,
and accepted compliments with red-lip smiles
of how ravishing they looked in their nurse's whites.

These visits could never be over fast enough
for me, but leaving always had obstacles
like appointments, bills, and prescriptions,
which left Dad alone to start his slow shuffle toward the door.
When everyone in reception and the front office could hear,
he'd look over one shoulder, wave, and say "Vote Republican!"

The Fall

In the ten years that I took care of Dad,
the future was clear as the day was long.
It was inevitable that there would be a fall.

A danger and obstacle to himself
in the way that he shuffled along,
in the ten years that I took care of Dad,

I worried and wagered to myself
that he'd trip over feet, not sure nor strong.
It was inevitable that there would be a fall,

if only because he lived by himself,
and I dreaded the day it would come along.
In the ten years that I took care of Dad,

of getting groceries and not fixing that shelf,
of telling him "Be careful!" all day long,
it was inevitable that there would be a fall.

The day came when, getting the mail by himself,
he took the tumble while shuffling along.
In the ten years that I took care of Dad,
It was inevitable that there would be a fall.

Last Drive

In the excitement of Dad's falling,
in my talking to the neighbor who found
him, perhaps flailing in slow motion,
trying to get up, to get his mail,
to get back to his apartment,
to get back to the day and night
routine of independence
that he loved so much,
in the excitement of rushing
to his apartment, past familiar
landmarks that measured time
of previous drives in reluctant units
of obligation, in the rush to respond
to the inevitable that had finally come,
I missed the last drive to Dad's,
a blurred beginning of the end.

Nursing Home

The first thing you notice
is the traffic in wheel chairs,
two-lane hallways packed
at rush hour to get to dinner.

But like an old French film,
something is wrong, something
is not moving, the rush hour
is not rushing, no reason for speed.

Some are parked against the wall,
engines muttering as an attendant
steps into an office for some papers.
Those sitting in the wheel chairs

look at you with deep disdain
for invading their world,
for being an alien who just stepped
through a time-warp into their hell,

for being a presence they had been,
for being the adult child who has
come to commit the committing
of no return, who is the cause

of the grand finale's commencing.
In the midst of these glares of hate,
you desperately search for Admissions,
to meet the person who has the papers

for you to sign as quickly as possible,
so you can get the hell out of there,
get on down the road, get on with life
until you must come back for visiting hours,

until, one day, far into the impossible future,
you must come back for more than a visit.

Do Not Resuscitate

Yes or No. If the resident is dying
do not resuscitate.

The admissions form efficiently
asks the basic question.

All I had to do was check the box.
Yes or No.

Yes, of course. We all have to go sometime.
No, of course. Death is to be delayed at all cost.

Yes.   It is time.
No.   Just a little more time.

Yes.   I am tired of taking care of him.
No.   He's my father for God's sake.

Yes.   If he doesn't care, why should I?
No.   Of course he cares. Of course I care.

Yes.   If not today, then tomorrow.
No.   Not today, maybe tomorrow.

Yes.
No.

Yes.
No.

Next question. Telephone hookup?
Yes.

Foley

The nurse said he had his Foley
stretched as far as it would go
as he headed for the bathroom,
forgetting that he was "hooked up."

I stood there in my own thoughts,
trying to avoid the picture
vividly and profoundly projected
on the screen inside my head.

Surely he had to feel something,
the stretch, the full extension,
it had to be noticeable,
noticeable in no uncertain terms.

I wondered in an aftermath
of disconnected thought, if
the Foley artist in movie-making
was a distant cousin to Dad's Foley,

creating a strange nexus
of catheter and cinema sound,
stretching the unbelievable
into believable disbelief.

My Pad

That's what he called it one day,
lying in his sick bed, denying the fall,
refusing to admit to his dislocated hip.

He simply wanted to go home,
back to the way things were,
back to a place where all made sense,
he wanted to go back to his pad.

Nobody said "my pad," any more,
but there was a time when it was cool,
when people stopped and listened

to Dad growl a nasty piano
boogie-woogie into the haze
and clink of smoke and ice,
back in a time when Dad was cool.

Now, he simply wanted to go home,
back to the way things were,
back to a place where all made sense,
"I just want to go back to my pad."

Rehab Team Meeting

I was invited to the weekly meeting
to hear about how Dad was eating,

and walking, and dealing with life,
and not. The team reports were rife

with facts and figures, jargon and jokes
of Dad's unfailing charms. Then they spoke

with shaking heads of his daily decline,
his utter unwillingness to follow the line

of therapy that could help him recover
and even, with time and work, discover

a new life built around his relocated hip.
But Dad had somehow decided that his hip

was a signal, that it was time to stop
this nonsense called "life," time to stop

this incessant care and feeding of the clock,
that somehow his sputtering engine, chock

full of broken parts was, indeed, grinding to a halt
one damn joint at a time, and he found no fault

in this new form of progress that didn't move
forward, this new type of rehab that didn't improve,

but just left him alone to lie where he may,
and let the chips fall at the end of the day.

Observing Pain

After his third operation
to reset his hip,
an operation that could
have been unnecessary
if only he did his therapy,

after his third operation,
his pain was palpable,
his cries of agony
were weak emissions
out of a gaping mouth.

           "Ahhhh . . . ."
Like a startled infant,
       first curled up in bed,
then, suddenly, opened wide:
       Fingers. Mouth. Eyes.
Then shut back down into a tight grip
       against some invisible attack.

All the while, all I could do
was stand there and watch.
Unable to fill out another form to fix things.
Just be there.
Useless.

Stepping Back into a Busy Hospital Hallway

It is amazing how life
has the audacity
to go on when Dad
just stepped into death.

Life just bare-faced goes on.
Schedules to meet.
People to see.
The world doesn't stop.

When I stepped out
of his hospital room
after seeing his dead body,
it was like stepping

into another dimension.

I saw things going on
all around me, but
they didn't quite register
in what felt "normal."

I had just been in a room
with death.
Now, I was in a hallway
with life.

Life and death.
Inside the room.
Outside the room.
Stepping back

into a busy hallway.

Poem of Medals

I remember a picture of Dad
in his Air Force uniform: hat
with clouds and thunderbolts,
bronze oak leaf rank,
and ribbons, rows of ribbons
like a poem of medals,
telling the story in symbols
of valor and days at war,
campaigns, and good conduct.
I read the strophes of color,
the accents of stars and clusters,
and perform an exegesis,
hoping to divine the true meaning
of the man in the picture.
I read the poem over and over,
my lips move with invisible words
that rhyme in reds and yellows
in anger and wonder.

Michael McDermott has published poems in *Bourgeon* (online), *Minimus, WordWrights!, phoebe, Cabin Fever (Idaho), The Federal Poet, Frantic Egg,* and *Rustling*s; a short story in *Minimus*; and various non-fiction pieces. He is also included on the CD *Poetry Alive at IOTA: The IOTA Poetry Series 10th Anniversary Reading.* He has served on editorial boards of *WordWrights!* and *GW Forum* and was a manuscript reader for the Word Works Washington Prize poetry contest. He was an occasional guest host of the long-running IOTA Poetry series (Arlington, VA) and has been a featured reader and active participant in the Washington DC area poetry readings including IOTA Poetry Series, Mariposa Poetry Series, and POESIS. He has an MFA from George Mason University.